# COMPETITION IN
# DEFENSE PROCUREMENT

## Studies in Defense Policy

SELECTED TITLES

# COMPETITION IN DEFENSE PROCUREMENT

*Donald L. Pilling*

## THE BROOKINGS INSTITUTION
*Washington, D.C.*

# FOREWORD

THE 1980s were marked by repeated attempts to reform the nation's weapons acquisition process. No single reform received more attention than proposals for more competition in procuring weapons. Competition figured prominently, for example, in the thirty-two acquisition improvement initiatives promulgated in 1981 by Frank C. Carlucci, who was then deputy secretary of defense. And the need for more competition became a matter of law in 1984, when Congress passed the Competition in Contracting Act (CICA), which mandated specific annual increases in the amount of Defense Department contract money obligated under competitive circumstances. So-called second-sourcing and leader-follower arrangements, both aimed at imparting more competition in the production of weapon systems, were used increasingly over the decade.

It was generally believed by Carlucci and others that competition would reduce the prices of supplies and services and help to fight rising costs. In this study, however, Captain Donald L. Pilling, USN, questions the analytical basis for that belief. His analysis shows that the commonly used data base for competition studies is inadequate and that the standard framework for analyzing those data is flawed. Policymakers do not gain enough insight into how and when to conduct competition for major weapon systems acquisition, and face the problem of distinguishing anecdotal from systemic evidence on previous competition experience. The author proposes both an alternative model for the analysis of competition and an approach to competition that more closely aligns the defense industry's incentives with the government's interests.

Captain Pilling is now serving as commander of a destroyer squadron. This study was completed while he was the Navy's 1985–86 federal executive fellow at Brookings. He is grateful to Howard Manetti, Martin Binkin, Thomas L. McNaugher, and Michael K. MccGwire for their support during the conduct of the study and to John D. Steinbruner for his comments on the manuscript. Kathryn Ho and Catherine Meehan provided administrative support; Vernon L. Kelley and Amy R. Waychoff verified the published sources.

Brookings is grateful to the Ford Foundation for funding for this study.

The views expressed in this book are those of the author and should not be ascribed to the persons or organizations whose assistance is acknowledged, to the U.S. Navy, or to the trustees, officers, or staff members of the Brookings Institution.

BRUCE K. MAC LAURY
*President*

*July 1989*
*Washington, D.C.*

# CONTENTS

# COMPETITION IN
# DEFENSE PROCUREMENT

# CHAPTER ONE

# COMPETITION IN THE DEFENSE MARKETPLACE

ECONOMISTS may debate the existence of markets to which the theory of free competition applies, but they generally agree that much of the theory does not apply to the defense marketplace.[1] Despite that consensus among analysts, managers in defense acquisition have consistently held that many commercial practices, including competition, will produce the same effects in defense procurement as in more conventional marketplaces.[2] Secretary of Defense Robert S. McNamara testified to Congress in 1965 that savings of 25 percent or more usually result from a conversion of sole-source procurement to competitive bidding.[3] The same conclusion was reached a decade later by J. Ronald Fox, a former assistant secretary of the army: "It seems reasonable to assume that a 25 percent reduction in a contract price can be achieved in many, if not most, cases when competition is

---

1. In a statement representative of this consensus, Peck and Scherer conclude that "a complete market system is an impossibility in the weapons acquisition process." Merton J. Peck and Frederic M. Scherer, *The Weapons Acquisition Process: An Economic Analysis* (Harvard University, Graduate School of Business Administration, Division of Research, 1962), p. 60. In his book *The Defense Industry* (MIT Press, 1980), pp. 30–31, Jacques S. Gansler lists two pages of differences between the defense market and a free market.

2. For example, a 1985 Navy initiative required defense contractors to finance the costs of production tooling, a practice previously limited to nongovernment commerce. Tooling costs have been the responsibility of government in defense contracts because of relatively high cost (several hundred million dollars for a major airframe production line) and to ensure that the government owns the tooling to move or restart the production line as necessary. See George C. Wilson and Michael Weisskopf, "Navy Orders Contractors to Buy Their Own Tools," *Washington Post*, November 21, 1985, p. A18; and Robert R. Ropelewski, "Aerospace Contractors Fault Navy Acquisition Proposal," *Aviation Week and Space Technology*, November 25, 1985, pp. 42–43.

3. Commander Benjamin R. Sellers, "Second Sourcing: A Way to Enhance Production Competition," *Program Manager*, vol. 12 (May–June 1983), p. 12.

introduced."[4] In 1981 Frank C. Carlucci, then deputy secretary of defense, made competition an article of faith in defense procurement by declaring it one of his thirty-two management initiatives for the new administration.

Although the reason most cited for introducing competition into defense procurement is that it reduces costs, the question answered least often about those lowered prices is, "Compared with what?" When a piece of hardware is initially procured under sole-source conditions, the introduction of a second source effectively destroys the sole-source environment; price levels under competition can then be compared only with the hypothetical prices that might have existed if competition hadn't been introduced. This problem is somewhat analogous to the Heisenberg uncertainty principle in physics, which states that certain experiments alter the parameters to be measured. That is, the belief that competition saves money is based on comparisons of hypothetical sole-source prices with actual prices obtained under competition.

An understanding of the mechanics of these comparisons reveals their weakness in providing insights for defense acquisition managers. Both the data and the analysis of the most frequently cited competition studies are questionable; the studies generally fail to account for the total costs of competition; and their models ignore the most relevant business strategies of the competitors.

## The Methodology

The calculations of savings from competitive bidding for defense goods are most often based on projections made from a "price improvement curve." This curve is developed from the change in price level experienced during the production of the item. The price improvement curve, in turn, is a generalization of the "learning curve," an analytical tool used by cost analysts. The learning curve is a statistically derived function that models direct manufacturing labor hours (not dollars) as a function of the cumulative number of units produced.[5] The concept of the learning curve arose from the analysis of the manufacturing hours required to produce

4. J. Ronald Fox, *Arming America: How the U.S. Buys Weapons* (Harvard University, Graduate School of Business Administration, Division of Research, 1974), p. 256.

5. The following explanation of the learning curve is based in part on Harold Asher, *Cost-Quantity Relationships in the Airframe Industry*, R-291 (Santa Monica, Calif.: Rand Corp., July 1, 1956), pp. 1–3, 15–17.

pre–World War II aircraft in the United States. It was observed that unit labor hours decreased at a logarithmic rate as the cumulative quantity of units produced increased. The functional form of the learning curve in that analysis of aircraft production is

$$M = AQ^b,$$

where $M$ represents the worker hours to produce the $Q$th airframe, $A$ is the worker hours required to produce the first airframe (the start point), and $b$ is a negative quantity related to the "slope" of the learning curve by the equation

$$\text{slope} = 2^b.$$

A slope of 90 percent means that the manufacturing hours needed to produce the second unit will be 90 percent of the hours needed for the first unit. Every subsequent doubling of the cumulative quantity would realize another 10 percent reduction in the hours required to produce one unit; for example, the fourth unit will require 90 percent of the hours of the second unit.

The concept of the learning curve is often expressed in terms of a worker becoming more efficient by performing the same task on successive units. However, this is only a first-order approximation of labor learning; many other factors are involved. For example, once production starts, gains may arise from improvements to the production line, to hand tools, or to the flow and distribution of parts to the production line.

The generalization to a price curve assumes that the effects of labor learning are so pervasive in determining the overall cost of an item that the logarithmic reduction in the worker hours required for one unit as modeled in a learning curve translates into the same logarithmic reduction in unit prices at the aggregate level. Keeping this generalization in mind, one can review the role of price curves in the savings calculations used for the historical studies of competition.

Savings from competition are typically calculated in a four-step procedure (figure 1-1):

—establish a sole-source curve based on the price levels of the purchases made before the introduction of competition;

—project this curve out to the relevant quantity to determine price levels for hypothetical future purchases in the absence of competition;

—compare these hypothetical sole-source price levels with the prices obtained under competition; and

**Figure 1-1. Cost Based on Hypothetical Sole-Source Learning Curve Compared with Estimated Savings When Competition Introduced**

Logarithmic scales

Thousands of fiscal dollars per unit

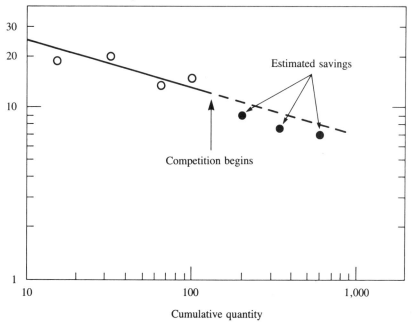

Cumulative quantity

—sum the savings for each purchase to obtain the total recurring savings for the entire program.

Costs that should be debited against these recurring savings are the nonrecurring costs required to establish a second source. Examples are the cost of a second set of production tooling and, as is often the practice in tactical missile procurement, the cost of an "educational" purchase of a small number of units from the second source to ensure that it can produce the hardware. Finally, the funding streams for both the hypothetical sole-source program and the competitive program being evaluated should be discounted to calculate savings in present-value terms.

## The Evidence

Applications of the above method can be seen in four studies that are representative of the procurement literature. The four studies—two written by government agencies and two by a federal contract research center—analyze several weapons systems or components and are the ones cited most frequently as evidence of savings available from production competition.[6] The source of the studies and their year of completion are as follows: the U.S. Army Electronics Command, 1972 (hereafter ECOM 72); the Institute for Defense Analyses, 1974 (IDA 74); the U.S. Army Procurement Research Office, 1978 (APRO 78); and the Institute for Defense Analyses, 1979 (IDA 79).[7]

The studies as a whole and individually are weak in several respects. As a whole, the studies overlap one another in the systems they analyze. The systems are not representative of major defense acquisitions. Of the forty-seven systems addressed in the four studies, thirty-one are electronic or electrical components. The remaining sixteen items are for guided missiles or munitions. Most of the items have an average price of less than $25,000. Twenty-one of the systems had either no sole-source or only one data point preceding competition (table 1-1). The IDA 79 study claimed to have excluded all these cases in its data base but nonetheless included in its analysis five systems that had only one sole-source procurement before competition.

The calculation of savings in each study is incomplete. ECOM 72 and IDA 74 for the most part considered only the prices bid on the first purchase after the initiation of competition, thereby excluding subsequent reprocurements, the nonrecurring costs of introducing competition, and subsequent claims against the government. Some of these costs were considered in APRO 78 and IDA 79. Unlike IDA 79, the APRO 78 calculations

---

6. Consulting firms that study competition are in high demand by program managers who must decide whether competition makes sense and, if it does, must choose the best competition strategy. The source documents for these systems-specific studies invariably tend to be similar to the four studies cited here.

7. U.S. Army Electronics Command, Cost Analysis Division, Comptroller, "The Cost Effects of Sole Source vs. Competitive Procurement," Fort Monmouth, N.J., February 1972; Morris Zusman and others, "A Quantitative Examination of Cost-Quantity Relationships: Competition during Procurement, and Military versus Commercial Prices for Three Types of Vehicles," IDA Paper S-429, vol. 2 (Arlington, Va.: Institute for Defense Analyses, March 1974); Edward T. Lovett and Monte G. Norton, "Determining and Forecasting Savings from Competing Previously Sole Source/Noncompetitive Contracts," APRO-709-03 (Fort Lee, Va.: U.S. Army Procurement Research Office, October 1978); and George G. Daly, Howard P. Gates, and James A. Schuttinga, "The Effect of Price Competition on Weapons System Acquisition Costs," IDA Paper P-1435, prepared for the Office of the Under Secretary of Defense for Research and Engineering (Arlington, Va.: Institute for Defense Analyses, Program Analysis Division, September 1979).

**Table 1-1. Systems and Extent of Sole-Source Procurement in Four Competition Studies**

| Type of system | | |
|---|---|---|
| *Electronic or electrical* | | *Missiles or munitions* |
| *Two or more lots under sole-source procurement* | | |
| CV-1548 | Aerno 42-0750 | TOW launcher |
| TD-204 | Aerno 60-6402 | TOW missile |
| AN/APM-123 | SPA-25 | Talos guidance and control |
| MD-522A/GRC | AN/PRT-4 | Bullpup AGM-12 B1 missile |
| TD-352 | TD-660 | Rockeye cluster bomb |
| USM-181 | AN/APX-72 | Standard missile |
| PPS-5 | FGC-20 | AIM-9D/G GCG |
| ARC-54 | Aerno 42-2028 | Shillelagh missile |
|  |  | Hawk metal motor parts |
|  |  | MK-46 torpedo |
| *Fewer than two lots under sole-source procurement* | | |
| AN/ARC-131 | MK-48 electric assembly | MK-48 warhead |
| AN/UPM-98 | FAAR radar | Shrike missile |
| PP-4763/GRC | FAAR TADDS | Dragon tracker |
| AN/PRC-25 | UPN-98 test set | Dragon round |
| TD-206/G | TD-202 | S-250/G shelter |
| AN/FYC-8X | AN/PRC-77 | AIM-9B GCG |
| AN/GRC-103 | AN/ASN-43 |  |
| AN/GRC-106 |  |  |

Source: ECOM 72, IDA 74, APRO 78, and IDA 79 studies; see text.

reflect the percentage saved against the entire production run, not just the competition portion. None of the studies discounted the funding streams. The results are as follows:[8]

| Study | Number of systems | Savings (percent) | |
|---|---|---|---|
|  |  | Mean | Range |
| ECOM 72 | 13 | 53.0 | 75.0 to    12.0 |
| IDA 74 | 20 | 36.8 | 60.3 to  −0.2 |
| APRO 78 | 16 | 10.8 | 51.0 to −13.2 |
| IDA 79 | 31 | 35.1 | 64.0 to −23.0 |

Thus the savings reported by these studies varied from a loss of 23

8. K. A. Archibald and others, *Factors Affecting the Use of Competition in Weapon System Acquisition,* R-2706-DR&E, prepared for the Office of the Under Secretary of Defense for Research and Engineering (Santa Monica, Calif.: Rand Corp., February 1981), pp. 32, 34, 38, 42.

percent to a gain of 75 percent. The Rand review of the four studies examined here found that, depending on the method of calculation, the estimate of savings on one system alone could vary by roughly the same 100-point range—for example, on the Shillelagh missile, from $-14$ percent to 79 percent.[9] Clearly, one can structure a basis for virtually any view on the benefits of competition if the data can yield such widely varied results.

Significant conceptual problems exist with the raw price data in the four studies. The studies use budgetary data rather than actual prices paid or costs to manufacturers; their selection of systems is skewed toward relatively inexpensive electronic components that experienced large variations in price not typically found in competition of major multimillion-dollar hardware items; and they include nonrecurring costs in the recurring price data for some systems. Further, many of the electronic components have commercial analogs and the competing producers had significant commercial business, so that analysis which ignores the increased labor learning and the commercial share of a plant's fixed overhead costs could produce misleading results.[10]

The failure to separate out nonrecurring costs involved with both the development of the system and the establishment of the initial production line artificially inflates early price levels and distorts projections of future prices. If a relatively flat slope is obtained from the preliminary data, it will yield an overestimate of future savings. Also, if the slope is steep, it will underestimate future savings resulting from competition. Again, if the slope is steep, very low future costs will be predicted, thus discouraging consideration of competition. Nonrecurring costs can be observed in the basic data used for the TOW missile and launcher, for the Dragon tracker and missile, and for the Shillelagh missile. The inability to discriminate between nonrecurring and recurring costs is typical of the financial data available for systems from the 1950s and the 1960s, the period of production for the forty-seven systems.

9. Archibald and others, *Factors Affecting the Use of Competition*, pp. 46–47.

10. Indeed, recent popular reporting of horror stories in defense procurement in the 1980s has concentrated not on major hardware procurements but on inexpensive commercial items. Toilet seats, coffee pots, and ashtrays have been held up as examples of high cost to the government because of mismanagement; in fact, their high cost was due to an arbitrary allocation of costs from a contract for a major end-item. If competition has value, then it should certainly be introduced for these common commercial items; competition for these awards should be the keenest because they require only a minimal manufacturing expertise and the barriers to entry in these markets are low.

### Analytical Problems

The use of a price curve demands a full understanding of the underlying mechanism, the learning curve. First, the learning curve was developed to model labor-intensive manufacturing on high-quantity production lines. An extension of the learning-curve model to highly automated activity or to low-quantity production such as shipbuilding is often made without an awareness of the conceptual flaws.

Second, early manufacturing experience, even for as long as a year, can be a poor predictor of the eventual labor requirements and learning-curve slope for the entire production run. In 1976 James Cullen studied seventy-nine aircraft programs for the Department of Defense (DOD). He concluded that the "eventual program learning curve slope cannot be predicted with any accuracy from initial actual cost data until approximately 8 data points exist. . . . As the data indicate, cost estimating from early actuals remains more of an art than a science and blind application of any given technique will undoubtedly result in substantial inaccuracies. Particular care must be taken in estimating from the first three actuals or in selecting a probable program learning curve from early data."[11] A data point represents the average worker hours per unit for a given production lot, and lot sizes can range from an entire year's production run to as many as four lots a year in the airframe industry. Thus several years of manufacturing experience may be required before a statistical projection of future manufacturing costs can be made with confidence.

Cullen's work on the number of data points necessary to predict with confidence the overall learning-curve slope (eight) and the dangers of using three or fewer points casts doubts on the usefulness of the results in the four studies examined here. The following table displays the number of data points under the sole-source conditions for each of the forty-seven systems:

---

11. J. S. Cullen, "Cost Estimating from Initial Actuals," paper prepared for the Office of the Director, Planning and Evaluation, Office of the Secretary of Defense, August 20, 1976, p. 16. Cullen studied the data on labor hours expended for seventy-nine aircraft production programs from the late 1940s (B-47) through the mid-1970s (F-14A) to find the amount of production required to determine a program learning curve with confidence. He showed that the variation between the eventual curve for a program and that generated by fitting early data points to a curve did not decrease until the first eight data points were used.

| Number of sole-source data points | Number of systems |
|---|---|
| 0–1 | 21 |
| 2–3 | 6 |
| 4–6 | 6 |
| 7 or more | 0 |
| Unable to determine from study data | 14 |
| All | 47 |

At best, the fourteen systems for which the number of data points is unknown—less than one-third of the systems studied—might have the eight or more points necessary for confidence in the projection of the price curve. More damaging is the fact that twenty-seven of the remaining thirty-three projections have three or fewer data points from which to make the projections.[12] With so few data points, these projections are likely to be inaccurate, and even a small inaccuracy would loom large in the results. For example, the variation between unit costs for a curve with a 78 percent slope and one with an 80 percent slope is 18 percent at 100 units, 21 percent at 200 units, and 23 percent at 300 units.[13]

With such a significant difference possible after only 300 units, one

12. The statistical arguments made here against projecting curves from a minimal amount of information are even more relevant when one considers competition models based on what might best be called the "shift and rotation" school of analysis, a method of curve adjustment frequently found in the literature on competition. It assumes that the price curve level drops (the "shift") and the slope steepens (the "rotation") once competition is introduced. To my knowledge the literature is devoid of examples that support this hypothesis. Moreover, one would be surprised to find such an example because the data requirements to verify the assumptions would be unprecedented—eight or more data points to establish the slope and level of the sole-source curve, and then eight or more to reflect the effect of competition. Even if one suspends the statistical argument and considers curves fitting with two or three data points, the assumption does not appear justified. For example, data on worker hours collected by Scherer for World War II aircraft show that in four of seven cases labor learning curves flattened out, not steepened, at the lead production facility after competitive second sources were established. See the discussion in Frederic M. Scherer, *The Weapons Acquisition Process: Economic Incentives* (Harvard University, Graduate School of Business Administration, Division of Research, 1964), pp. 119–26. Even when considered at the price level, the hypothesis appears false (for example, price curve slopes flattened on the Bullpup, AIM-9D G&C, and Shillelagh programs after competition began). Further, it can be argued that the rate of production, fixed overhead costs, and the use by the second source of the lead source's vendors have a much greater influence on price levels than the competition itself.

13. Cullen, "Cost Estimating from Initial Actuals," p. 16.

can appreciate how much error can be introduced into a calculation projecting from three or fewer data points onto production runs with thousands of units. According to APRO 78, for the systems considered, the average quantity of units procured after competition was introduced was 19,443 units, ranging from a low of 85 for FAAR radars to 247,098 for TOW missiles.

Another weakness in the linkage between learning curves and price curves is that little empirical evidence exists to support a change in the slope or level of a learning curve (as opposed to a price curve) to estimate the cost effect of a change in production rate. Price curves address costs at the aggregate level of total unit price and include a prorated level of fixed production costs such as fixed overhead, engineering support, and program management costs. Each production unit carries a share of these costs, so its price is closely tied to the production rate. This strongly suggests that the reliance of the price curve on an underlying learning-curve theory is inappropriate.[14]

### Contractor Behavior

Another type of problem with the competition studies is that they assume no price effect exists preceding the onset of competition. However, Michael Beltramo has noted that in six of forty-six systems examined, the price of the last buy procured under sole-source conditions was much

---

14. A Rand report concluded that "the effect of production rate on manufacturing labor . . . cannot be predicted with confidence." Joseph P. Large, Karl Hoffmayer, and Frank Kontrovich, *Production Rate and Production Cost,* R-1609-PA&E, report prepared for the Assistant Secretary of Defense (Program Analysis and Evaluation) (Santa Monica, Calif.: Rand Corp., December 1974), p. 41. At the level of price versus labor hours, argued Groemping, Large and others would have observed the effect of the production rate had they considered the *aggregate* cost of manufacturing labor, manufacturing materials, tooling, and engineering. Ralph A. Groemping, "Production Rate Is Important," TP-1061 (J. Watson Noah Associates, December 1976). That is exactly the point being made here: one cannot predict with certainty the effect of the production rate at the level of learning curves; but once the level of aggregation includes these other costs, the production rate becomes very important. More recently, econometricians who have attempted to link microeconomic theory with learning curve theory have concluded that production rate changes do influence learning curves if analyzed within the context of "diminishing returns on discounted program costs." Thomas R. Gulledge, Jr., and Norman K. Womer, *The Economics of Made-to-Order Production: Theory with Applications Related to the Airframe Industry,* Lecture Notes in Economics and Mathematical Systems 261 (New York: Springer–Verlag, 1986), p. 31.

below the learning-curve slope.[15] The reasons for this phenomenon are unknown, but conceivably the sole-source manufacturer adopted a pre-competition pricing strategy to convince the DOD program manager that competition was unnecessary.[16] Conversely, Beltramo found three instances in which prices went up significantly for the sole-source lots just before competition. In these cases the manufacturer may have been taking profits early in anticipation of split procurements.[17] Price analyses of subsequent savings in any of these cases would mistake the institutional behavior of the contractor struggling to get business for the workings of the price curve. This masking of contractor behavior is evident in the analysis of the Sparrow (AIM-7F) missile competition.[18]

The Sparrow air-to-air missile is a medium-range weapon used by Navy and Air Force fighter aircraft. The AIM-7F series of the Sparrow was in full production in the second half of the 1970s. The AIM-7F component placed under competitive procurement was the guidance and control hardware, which represents about 90 percent of the total price of the missile. The prices paid by the government to the two contractors—Raytheon, which was the developer and initial production source, and General Dynamics (GD)—are shown in table 1-2. The two early GD lots of 15 and 70 units were educational purchases required to ensure that GD could satisfactorily produce the hardware. The first competitive purchase was in fiscal year 1977, with Raytheon winning the award of 1,110 guidance and control units and GD winning a smaller award of 210 units.

A plot of the prices charged by Raytheon and General Dynamics versus cumulative quantity raises several issues (figure 1-2). Although the data are purportedly for recurring prices only, the steepness of the Raytheon

15. See Michael N. Beltramo, "A Case Study of the Sparrow AIM-7F," *Program Manager,* vol. 14 (September–October 1985), pp. 28–35.

16. A Tecolote Research analysis of costs for systems engineering and program management for tactical missile systems concluded that "contractors organize their accounting procedures and apply their resources in a competitive posture, when competition is perceived to be likely." Analysis at the aggregate price level would miss these changes going on inside the contractor's plant. C. A. Graver and S. P. Hu, "Competition Impacts on System Engineering and Program Management Cost Factors in Air Force and Navy Missile Programs," TR-004, report prepared for the Department of Defense Joint Cruise Missiles Project, Tecolote Research, Santa Barbara, Calif., July 1985, p. 3.

17. R. Berg, R. Dennis, and J. Jandrow called this "anticipation hypothesis" in "Price Analysis and the Effects of Competition," Professional Paper 442 (Alexandria, Va.: Center for Naval Analyses, October 1985), pp. 15–16.

18. In making my analysis of the AIM-7F cost data, I relied on Beltramo, "Case Study of the Sparrow AIM-7F," for chronology.

**Table 1-2. Recurring Production Prices of Competitors for the Guidance and Control System of the AIM-7F Missile**

Fiscal 1977 dollars

| | Raytheon | | | General Dynamics | | |
|---|---|---|---|---|---|---|
| *Fiscal year* | *Number of units* | *Average cost (thousands of dollars)* | *Total cost (millions of dollars)* | *Number of units* | *Average cost (thousands of dollars)* | *Total cost (millions of dollars)* |
| 1972 | 100 | 416 | 41.6 | ... | ... | ... |
| 1973 | 225 | 212 | 47.7 | 15 | 917 | 13.7 |
| 1975 | 600 | 112 | 67.0 | 70 | 233 | 16.3 |
| 1976 | 880 | 95 | 83.3 | 210 | 130 | 27.3 |
| 1977 | 1,110 | 75 | 83.2 | 210 | 107 | 22.5 |
| 1978 | 1,400 | 65 | 91.1 | 750 | 78 | 58.1 |
| 1979 | 900 | 62 | 55.9 | 1,310 | 52 | 68.6 |
| 1980 | 1,144 | 54 | 61.2 | 300 | 69 | 20.6 |
| Total | 6,359 | ... | 531.0 | 2,865 | ... | 227.1 |

Source: Michael N. Beltramo, "A Case Study of the Sparrow AIM-7F," *Program Manager*, vol. 14 (September–October 1985), pp. 28–35.

slope (about 70 percent) for the first three lots suggests that some non-recurring costs may be buried in the prices charged for these early lots. A missile production run is unlikely to sustain a price improvement slope of more than 80 percent. If the steep slope was caused by the impending competition, then the best government option would have been to keep threatening competition without actually introducing it. That strategy would both continue the steep price improvement and achieve the economies of scale inherent in a single producer versus split production!

A regression of the data for the first four Raytheon lots (the actual competition began with the fifth lot) yields a slope of 84 percent, a much more reasonable figure and consistent with Raytheon's experience on the AIM-7C, a predecessor of the AIM-7F. The price curve methodology requires a projection of this slope as a sole-source basis for measuring savings. This projection shows that the dual-source competition actually *lost* money; that is, the total recurring price for the two producers ($758 million) was $88 million, or 13 percent, higher than it would have been if the initial source, Raytheon, had produced the entire quantity at an 84 percent slope. The loss is due primarily to the flattening of Raytheon's price improvement slope beginning with the purchase for fiscal year 1977 and to the fact that GD was able to beat Raytheon's price in one year only (fiscal year 1979).

**Figure 1-2. Prices Charged by Competitors for the Guidance and Control System of the AIM-7F Missile, by Cumulative Quantity**

Logarithmic scales

Thousands of fiscal dollars per unit

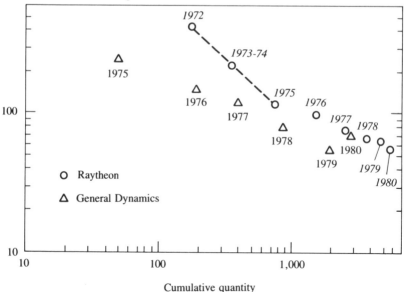

Cumulative quantity

   The flattening of the Raytheon price curve is an example of the anticipation hypothesis described earlier. Raytheon doubled its profit (from 13 percent to 25 percent) in the early stages of the competition when GD was unable to beat Raytheon's prices. It also appears that GD may have lost money in the year it won the majority award (fiscal 1979) because GD raised its prices the following year (fiscal 1980).

   Considering the nonrecurring costs associated with GD's effort to qualify as a second source, competition was even more costly. A total of $38.7 million was required for the preparation of data, and for planning, tooling, and test equipment. Added to the $88 million recurring price loss, the actual percentage increase in production price was 19 percent ($88 million recurring and $39 million nonrecurring over a $670 million sole-source cost).

   Contractor behavior is masked by analysis at the price level. Examination of the detailed cost shows that Raytheon was able to meet the GD competition by reducing manufacturing support costs. Raytheon's plant

**Figure 1-3. Government Purchases and Vendor Deliveries of the Guidance and Control System for the AIM-7F Missile by Two Competitors, 1973–83[a]**

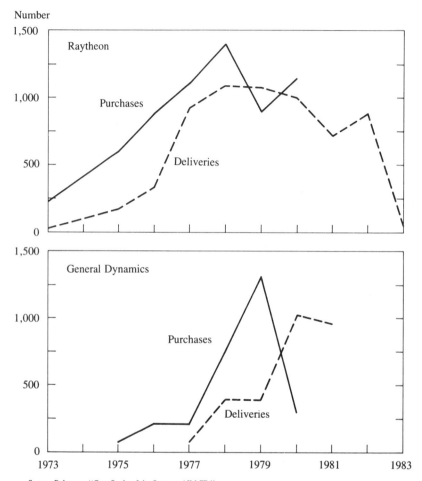

Source: Beltramo, "Case Study of the Sparrow AIM-7F."
a. The delivery data for the Raytheon lot of 100 missiles (fiscal 1972) and the GD lot of 15 missiles (fiscal 1973–74) are not available.

in Lowell, Massachusetts, where the units for the AIM-7F were produced, was concurrently producing Sidewinder/AIM-9 missiles, and in fiscal 1977 the plant had a production run under the foreign military sales program of 983 AIM-7E/7H missiles. Analyzing hardware costs for a single product line in isolation would miss a contractor's ability to shift manufacturing support personnel to other programs in the plant when faced with competition. Similarly, the business base of the GD plant included production of the Standard/RIM-67 missile, which must be considered in determining how GD was able to set its prices.

Another aspect of contractor behavior that the competition studies overlook is the contractor's ability to negotiate delivery schedules to smooth the work load rather than be subject to the radical swings in annual production suggested by the competitive awards shown in table 1-2. Figure 1-3 is the schedule of deliveries by the two contractors. It reflects Raytheon's success in maintaining reasonably stable production rates to guarantee stability of the work force, one of management's tools to ensure worker satisfaction and productivity and a determinant of pricing not considered by the competition studies.

### Final Observations

The evidence fails to demonstrate statistically that procurement competition does in fact reduce program cost. Competition in the AIM-7F program actually increased costs. The strongest conclusion that can be drawn from the data is a very limited one. In ten of the fifteen systems for which a procurement followed the first competitive award, prices did not go up. This suggests that competition should be considered more of a cost *avoidance* measure than a cost *reduction* device.

If the theory underlying the price curve methodology is correct, the initial producer, if competent, should virtually always win a head-to-head competition with a second source because the labor force of the first producer and of that producer's vendors are further down the learning curve. However, the initial producer won head-to-head competition in only one of seventeen systems examined in the IDA 74 study. This result indicates that fundamental price curve theory is flawed for analysis of competition, or initial producers tend to maintain a potentially inefficient manufacturing strategy despite being faced with competition (and perhaps choose instead to pursue only a change in pricing strategy). In either case, the results of competition are unpredictable under the price curve methodology.

As the Rand study by Archibald concluded, ''The existing body of analysis has not provided an adequate set of management tools for estimating the benefits or the costs of competitive reprocurement. . . . Existing research provides neither quantitative nor qualitative guidance for designing price competitive reprocurement strategies.''[19] Similarly, a review of the competition literature by the Center for Naval Analyses found that analysis based on the simple price improvement curve ''ignores too many factors to be of much use in evaluating the effects of competition on prices.''[20]

19. Archibald and others, *Factors Affecting the Use of Competition*, pp. 53, 57.
20. Berg and others, ''Price Analysis,'' p. 17.

# CHAPTER TWO

# OTHER ASPECTS OF COMPETITION

BEYOND the issue of cost, competition offers several potential advantages over sole-source procurement, some of which appear to have been realized, some not. Additional benefits cited by Deputy Secretary of Defense Carlucci in 1981 were improved contractor responsiveness, increases in the industrial base, and fairness of opportunity. This chapter examines these benefits and provides examples of two industries in which competition has produced mixed results.

## Contractor Responsiveness

For analytical purposes, contractor responsiveness can be measured in terms of improved quality, adherence to contractual schedules, and reduced cost overruns.[1] Within these parameters, the evidence indicates that competition has had some success in cases that required evaluation of prototype hardware before the initiation of a full-scale development. A 1979 Rand study compared such programs with those in which either no competition or limited competition based on paper designs was held (table 2-1).[2] The study, which must be considered only suggestive because of its small sample size, supports the intuitive belief that prototype hardware competition confers some benefits. The Rand study noted that in three of the four prototype hardware programs, the winning development contractor was not the same one that would have been selected if only paper designs had been evaluated. The study did not attempt to quantify the

---

1. Contractor responsiveness from a qualitative perspective is difficult. See the appendix to this chapter.

2. Edmund Dews and others, *Acquisition Policy Effectiveness: Department of Defense Experience in the 1970's*, R-2516-DR&E (Santa Monica, Calif.: Rand Corp., October 1975).

**Table 2-1. Comparison of Contractor Performance, Competitive Awards and Noncompetitive Awards**

| | *Ratio of results to goals[a]* | |
|---|---|---|
| *Performance criteria* | *Competitive awards[b]* | *Noncompetitive awards[c]* |
| System performance | 0.98 | 1.07 |
| Program schedule | 1.06 | 1.17 |
| Program cost | | |
| Range | 0.87–1.27 | 1.24–2.12 |
| Mean | 1.16 | 1.53 |

Source: Edmund Dews and others, *Acquisition Policy Effectiveness: Department of Defense Experience in the 1970's*, R-2516-DR&E (Santa Monica, Calif.: Rand Corp., October 1975).

a. System performance, program schedule, and program cost results were calculated by comparing actual results with initial estimates.

b. Four aircraft programs: AWACS, A-10, F-16, UH-60.

c. Six aircraft, missile, mine and vehicle programs: F-15, Aegis, Harpoon, AIM-9L, CAPTOR, M-198.

benefits in these cases, but it concluded that a better weapon system resulted from prototype hardware systems.[3]

Whether a contractor's responsiveness improves when a formerly sole-source procurement is put out for bid is more difficult to assess. In 1983 Michael Beltramo studied this issue with regard to major weapons systems procured during the 1960s and 1970s.[4] He examined the technical, management, labor, and capital factors that led to program disruptions, such as schedule delays and cost overruns in defense acquisition programs. Observing that disturbances such as union strikes and vendor nonperformance would have affected all the prime contractors competing for an end-item, he concluded that though a second source might lessen some risks connected with production, those risks are not the main causes of poor performance, delays in schedule, or cost overruns. Starting up a second source is no guarantee that performance, schedule, or cost problems will be eliminated.

Other studies of specific systems also indicate that goals for quality, schedule, and cost were not met despite competition. A Naval Air Systems Command study surveyed six tactical missile programs produced under

3. The principle of requiring prototype hardware before full-scale development ("fly before buy") was an initiative instituted by Deputy Secretary of Defense David Packard in the early 1970s. It was reaffirmed recently in the Packard-led Presidential Blue Ribbon Commission on Defense Management, *An Interim Report to the President*, February 28, 1986, p. 17. (Hereafter Blue Ribbon Report.)

4. Michael N. Beltramo, *Dual Production Sources in the Procurement of Weapon Systems: A Policy Analysis*, P-6911-RGI (Santa Monica, Calif.: Rand Corp., November 1983).

competitive procurement during the 1960s.[5] Four of the winning contractors won subsequent claims against the government for costs associated with production problems resulting from inadequate data packages; the fifth contractor incurred a $16 million overrun that was not claimed against the government; and the sixth winner eventually required the original manufacturer's engineers to provide on-site assistance at government expense to solve manufacturing problems and improve quality. Although one could argue that this is a criticism of government competitive procedures, not of competition itself, it does illustrate that the benefits of competition do not accrue simply by holding a competition.

The studies reviewed in chapter 1 also contained evidence that competition actually introduced rather than prevented problems of quality and cost in some programs. The IDA 74 study observed that competition imposed costs and disruptions in the Bullpup program when the second source could not produce the weapon's nose cone.[6] In the APRO 78 study, five of the sixteen winners overran their contracts, and one program was severely disrupted when the contractor went out of business.[7]

## The Industrial Base

Whether the country's industrial base can sustain a rapid buildup to support a global war is a central issue of national security. Can competitive procurement be said to expand the size of the industrial base? It appears that if the competition is through dual sourcing the same product, the industrial capacity to produce the product is expanded, perhaps in excess of peacetime procurement levels. If the competition is for a single producer in a winner-take-all competition, the capacity to produce the product may actually decline.

The U.S. defense industry is divided into two levels, an upper (the

5. Report by Terry Rucker, December 1977, cited in Beltramo, *Dual Production Sources,* pp. 49, 50.

6. Morris Zusman and others, ''A Quantitative Examination of Cost-Quantity Relationships: Competition during Procurement, and Military versus Commercial Prices for Three Types of Vehicles,'' IDA Paper S-429, vol. 2 (Arlington, Va.: Institute for Defense Analyses, March 1974).

7. Edward T. Lovett and Monte G. Norton, ''Determining and Forecasting Savings from Competing Previously Sole Source/Noncompetitive Contracts,'' APRO-709-3 (Fort Lee, Va.: U.S. Army Procurement Research Office, U.S. Army Logistics Management Center, October 1978).

major, or primary, contractors) and a lower (the subcontractors and vendors). Over the past twenty-five years, the pool of primary defense contractors has changed very little (other than through mergers and acquisitions that created, for example, McDonnell-Douglas and North American–Rockwell). In the airframe industry, only North American–Columbus dropped out of the business in that period. A similar situation exists in shipbuilding. One change in this sector is that government yards now only repair ships instead of constructing them. Among the private yards, the shipbuilding division of Ingalls has dropped out, leaving only two shipyards capable of building nuclear submarines. Declining commercial business threatens to undermine the stability of other major shipbuilding yards.

The stability exhibited in the tier of prime contractors since the 1960s is not surprising given the enormous capitalization and technical sophistication required to produce modern weapons. Because of these high barriers to entry in this tier, it does not seem very likely that more intensive competition at the prime-contractor level will expand the number of primes.[8] Indeed, expansion of the base through dual-source competition would appear to be inefficient—as the Department of Defense would be paying the price of sustaining the excess capacity arising from two firms producing the same product. Either competition through dual sourcing for a product is inefficient or, if efficient, the industrial base can support only the peacetime requirement for that product. That Carlucci's goals for competition (reduce prices and broaden the base) were contradictory went largely unnoticed.

The number of defense firms in the second tier appears to have declined since the 1960s, a trend that began during the wind-down of the Vietnam War. However, the actual figures are debatable and so is the effect on those figures by dramatically higher defense spending and an increased number of competitive programs during the Reagan administration. Writing just before the onset of the Reagan era, former deputy assistant sec-

---

8. The case of the antiradiation missile (ARM) seekers shows that competition can have unpredictable results on the industrial base. The early ARM seekers (the Shrike series) were produced under competition between Texas Instruments (TI) and Sperry-Rand during the 1960s. After the first few years, Sperry-Rand dropped out of the business because TI's aggressive pricing of Shrike seekers made the market very unattractive; that is, aggressive competition reduced the base to one contractor. Later the Navy decided against competitive procurement for the current ARM seeker (the HARM missile) because the nonrecurring costs were too high to justify it, thereby leaving the field to TI. As a result, the potential second source, Bendix, chose to get out of the defense business entirely, because there was no opportunity to compete. In each case, competition and the lack of it narrowed the industrial base.

retary of defense Jacques Gansler observed that the number of active aerospace subcontractors had decreased from more than 6,000 in 1968 to fewer than 4,000 in 1975. He concluded that in the defense industry the nation has enough surge capacity at the prime level but does not have enough at the subcontractor level.[9] Gansler's analysis overlooks the fact that true defense subcontractors are extremely difficult to identify, so their numbers may not have declined. It also implies that increased competition could have expanded the base without demonstrating how, whereas one can argue from first principles that competition would have further narrowed the base.

At the time Gansler was writing his book, the Rand Corporation had just completed a study of the lower tier of the defense industrial base.[10] Although the conclusions were often tentative because of limited samples, the authors did determine that prime contractors experience little difficulty in finding alternative suppliers if one supplier should fail to perform. The reason for the fluctuation in the number of subcontractors was that many moved in and out of the industry as a function of the business available and of the potential gains to be realized from commercial spin-offs of the frequently highly specialized defense products. The frequent entry and exit is made possible by the relatively low barriers to such movement for the defense subcontracting industry. The Rand study also found that the number of vendors was being reduced by the vertical integration of the prime contractors, a trend in the defense industry over the last few decades. Vertical integration does not narrow the industrial base, but ignoring this

9. Jacques S. Gansler, *The Defense Industry* (MIT Press, 1980).

10. Genesse G. Baumbusch and Alvin J. Harman, *Peacetime Adequacy of the Lower Tiers of the Defense Industrial Base,* R-2184/1-AF (Santa Monica, Calif.: Rand Corp., November 1977). The authors failed to discriminate between competition as a technique to combat rising prices and as a method to reduce prices. They pointed out, "Our evidence concerning excessive prices as a measure of sufficient competition in the lower tiers of the industrial base is the least conclusive of any derived from our survey" (p. 25). Nonetheless, on the basis of two cases, they still concluded that "increasing competition does lead to lower prices" (p. 41). In the first case, the RF-4 ejector system, a contractor bought exclusive rights to the design of another contractor and then more than doubled the prices it had been charging. The Air Force was able to buy the design package, qualify a second source, and obtain more reasonable prices. In the second case, General Electric reversed the increasing trend of its prices for rocket motors after the prime contractor, Boeing, threatened to allow Thiokol to compete as an alternative producer of the motors. Both examples demonstrate that competition can help to avoid excessively high or rising prices; they do not demonstrate that competition reduces program costs relative to sole-source procurement in which the seller makes a reasonable profit and does not indulge in price gouging.

fact by simply counting the number of vendors then and now would lead one to the opposite conclusion.

More recently, a 1984 survey on the health of the subcontractor base in the shipbuilding industry and in aircraft manufacture reaffirmed that identification of "true" defense subcontractors is extremely difficult.[11] The study confirmed the earlier Rand conclusions that the shape and size of the second tier is poorly defined but that it is apparently healthy enough for peacetime needs.

The contribution of competition to the size of the industrial base remains unclear. The issue of increasing the number of prime contractors through dual-source versus winner-take-all competition has already been addressed. Significantly greater competition exists in the second tier. Of the contracts examined in the 1984 survey mentioned above, the prime contractors competed on 78 percent of their subcontracts. As a comparison, the Navy, the most vigorous of the services in instituting competition, had increased its rate of competitive awards to primes from 29 percent in 1981 to only 69 percent by 1985.

A final observation on the role of competition in sustaining the industrial base is its surprising *absence* from the testimony of Secretary of Defense Caspar Weinberger before the House Appropriations Committee hearings for fiscal 1986:

> Defense mobilization studies show that the industrial base supporting current defense procurements has been adequate in recent years. Under the stewardship of Department of Defense programs, current military needs are being met at lower costs and delays in procurement are being greatly reduced. . . . Programs for maximizing mobilization and surge capacities for the least amount of investment on the parts of the producer and DoD must continue. . . . Such programs include: (1) modernization of the production base for defense programs; (2) measures for emergency production acceleration; and (3) sustaining sufficient numbers of producers of critical items to meet security requirements.[12]

11. Keith S. Holtsclaw, *Capital Investment Motivational Techniques Used by Prime Contractors on Subcontractors* (Monterey, Calif.: Naval Post Graduate School, December 1984).

12. *Department of Defense Appropriations for 1986,* Hearings before a Subcommittee of the House Committee on Appropriations, 99 Cong. 1 sess. (GPO, 1985), pt. 1, p. 198.

**Fairness**

Of all the benefits of competition, fairness is clearly the most elusive to analyze because fairness is not quantifiable. Common sense suggests that the increased emphasis on competition has made it tougher for the DOD to be unfair to potential contractors by maintaining exclusive relationships with long-standing producers.

The aircraft wheel and brake industry is one example of a closed market that was allowed to exist before the current regulations on competition were legislated. Production had been dominated by three firms: Goodrich, Goodyear, and Bendix. Some small firms have acted as suppliers of replacement parts such as brake pads. One such small firm, Nasco, made a corporate decision in the 1970s to become a full-fledged developer-producer of wheel and brake systems by initially expanding into a full line of replacement parts. Since it and other small firms were lower priced than the three major firms, the expanding competition led Goodyear to threaten to get out of the military business unless the Air Force took exceptional measures. In response, the Air Force invoked a rule under the Armed Services Procurement Regulations that the service can forgo competitive bids in favor of negotiations with a single contractor (Goodyear in this case) if the service can demonstrate its necessity in preserving vital industrial capacity. The Air Force preference for a sole-source relationship with Goodyear, as demonstrated by its invocation of the procurement rule, led Nasco to abandon its plans to become a developer-producer of whole systems.[13] The irony is that a rule intended to maintain industrial capacity was used to suppress its expansion.

Under the new rules of competition imposed in 1981 (and formalized by the Competition in Contracting Act of 1984), an exception to the procurement regulations now is much more difficult to obtain. It also appears that the influence of the three major firms in the wheel and brake business has diminished considerably. An example of the discomfiture of the three major firms under the new regulations is a 1983 letter from the Goodyear Aircraft and Wheel Division to the Air Force arguing that competition for components of the wheel and brake system is unfair.[14]

---

13. For a fuller description, see Baumbusch and Harman, *Peacetime Adequacy of the Lower Tiers*.

14. Letter from A. A. Frederick, Business Development Rep, Aircraft and Wheel Division, Goodyear Aerospace Corporation, Akron, Ohio, of March 24, 1983, to U.S. Air Force Competition Advocate, Ogden Air Logistics Center.

The letter acknowledged that firms such as Goodyear use a buy-in strategy of low bids on development contracts, the losses on which are to be made up later on the production contracts. The potentially smaller production runs arising from split procurements will force Goodyear's vendors to recover all their development costs on the initial procurement. Under the current rules, another attempt by the Air Force to maintain an exclusive group of developer-suppliers in the wheel and brake business would be much more difficult to accomplish than it was in the case of Nasco.

## Summary

The following conclusions can be drawn from the evidence on the nonprice benefits of competition:

—Competition has proved an effective management tool in programs in which prototype hardware was evaluated before a commitment to full-scale development. However, once production has been initiated, effects of competition on quality, schedule, and cost are mixed.

—No evidence supports the belief that effective competition contributes to the expansion of the industrial base for defense procurement. Second sourcing does ensure that several contractors are capable of producing a given system, but it can result in excess capacity and increased costs.

—The increased emphasis on competition since 1981 has made the defense acquisition system more fair by increasing the difficulty for DOD buyers to maintain exclusive relationships with certain suppliers.

The general conclusion that can be drawn thus far on all the purported benefits of competition in defense procurement is that few clearcut insights exist for policymakers. The most disturbing finding is that inasmuch as military departments are essentially in competition among themselves to see which of them can achieve a greater percentage of contracts awarded competitively, competition may have become the end and not a means.[15]

15. For example, the Navy was the most successful and increased its percentage of contract dollars awarded competitively from 25 percent in fiscal 1981 to 45 percent in fiscal 1985, with a goal of 51 percent in fiscal 1986. In terms of contract actions awarded competitively, the percentage increased from 29 percent in fiscal 1981 to 69 percent in fiscal 1985. A good example of money being spent to achieve dual-source competition was the Phoenix missile program, in which $237.9 million was invested to qualify a second source. Navy officials have admitted that this nonrecurring cost would not be recovered. *Department of Defense Appropriations for 1986*, pt. 4, p. 362.

This issue was recognized by the Packard Commission when it stated, "Common sense, the indispensable ingredient for a successful system, has not always governed acquisition strategies. More competition, for example, is beneficial, but the mechanistic pursuit of competition for its own sake would be inefficient and sacrifice quality—with harmful results."[16] The Packard Commission was silent, however, on the means by which the DOD could attain a competitive environment yielding quality products, on time, and at a reasonable cost. Indispensable to such an environment is DOD sensitivity to the behavioral aspects of the unique buyer-seller relationships in the defense marketplace and the constantly changing nature of the prime contractor's manufacturing operations. The next chapter will address the behavioral issue and the changing character of the modern production line.

### Appendix: Two Case Studies of Competition

The use of competition in acquisition programs to reduce program costs, improve contractor performance, increase the industrial base, and ensure fairness of opportunity are examined here in two case studies. They illustrate the difficulty of getting clearcut evidence on the benefits of competition. The two are the Air Force's fighter engine competition, which pitted against each other for the F-15/F-16 fighter engine business Pratt & Whitney (P&W) and General Electric (GE), the two primary jet engine manufacturers in the United States; and the U.S. shipbuilding industry's competition for the shrinking shipbuilding–ship repair business. Both examples demonstrate why avid supporters of competition conclude that counterexamples of their beliefs on the benefits of competition are special cases, when in fact the converse may be true.

### *The Great Fighter Engine Competition*

Pratt & Whitney developed the F-100 engine for the F-15 aircraft in the early 1970s. In a precursor of problems that would develop later, the high-performance engine failed its first military qualification test (MQT) in September 1973 because it could not complete the required 100-hour endurance test. The F-15 program manager authorized the go-ahead on

16. Blue Ribbon Report, p. 15.

engine production despite the failure, arguing that the F-15 development and production schedule could not absorb a slip. The engine successfully completed its MQT in December 1973.

As is common practice for military engine programs, the Air Force subsequent to the MQT continued to spend money on development of the F-100 through the F-100 Component Improvement Program (CIP). Between 1972 and 1985 this program spent over $500 million on three major components to improve the reliability of the engine. The three new components are in the F-100/PW-220 version of the engine, which was the P&W entry in the engine competition.[17]

The other major program in the early 1970s to develop a high-performance engine was General Electric's F-101 engine for the B-1 bomber. The F-101 benefited from technology advances subsequent to the F-100 and did not push the state of the art to the degree the F-100 did. With the cancellation of the B-1 program in 1977, GE found itself with an engine but no aircraft for it.

The Air Force was not comfortable with its sole-source relationship on the F-100 engine for the F-15 and, subsequently, F-16 aircraft. The problems with the F-100, the Air Force perception of P&W's indifference to solving them, and P&W's reluctance to provide significant warranties provided the initial impetus to develop a fighter version of the F-101 engine.[18] Air Force funding for the fighter version of the F-101 began in fiscal 1979. The GE approach was to use the F-101 core and scale up components from the F-404 engine, a smaller engine GE developed in the late 1970s for the Navy's F-18 fighter. Initial estimates of development cost were low, said as late as 1982 to be approximately $120 million.[19] Nonetheless, the derivative engine that was developed, called the F-110, eventually required $361 million in nonrecurring cost through fiscal 1985 to qualify for the competition.[20]

17. *Defense Department Authorization and Oversight,* Hearings on H.R. 5167 before the Committee on Armed Services, 98 Cong. 2 sess. (GPO, 1984), pt. 2, pp. 213–56.

18. A study from the John F. Kennedy School of Government documents through interviews with Air Force and P&W personnel the growing frustration of the Air Force with what it felt was P&W's lack of response to the F-100's problems. The F-101 (later the F-110) development was actually started as a low-cost demonstration program to persuade P&W that the Air Force had alternatives. See David M. Kennedy, "The Great Engine War," Kennedy School of Government Case Study C16-85-629 (Harvard University, 1985).

19. *Department of Defense Appropriations for Fiscal 1983,* Hearings before a Subcommittee of the Senate Committee on Appropriations, 97 Cong. 2 sess. (GPO, 1983), pt. 4, p. 30.

20. *Defense Department Authorization and Oversight,* Hearings on H.R. 5167, pt. 2., p. 223.

Pratt & Whitney countered the F-110 competition by claiming it was unfair. R. J. Carlson, the president of P&W, told Congress in 1982 that P&W's share of the commercial jet engine business had declined from roughly 65 percent of the market to 40 percent, a level comparable to that of GE.[21] He then argued that in the military engine business P&W had the advantage in large engines and GE the advantage in small engines. He displayed a forecast of business in military engines for the next ten years that showed GE with the larger share of the military market without the F-100/F-110 competition. Awarding F-15/F-16 engine business to GE would give it an even larger market share at the expense of P&W and would give GE an unfair advantage over P&W for future engine business.[22]

The competition was held nonetheless. The results depicted in table 2-2 were provided to Congress by the Air Force in 1984. Two critical points to note:

1. The Air Force chose to display life cycle costs, not procurement costs. The rationale was that the real savings from the competitive program were in the reduction of maintenance costs because both the F-110 and the improved F-100 were much more reliable engines. A reduction of one maintenance man-hour per equivalent flying hour was said to save approximately $1 billion. The competing engines were estimated to save $3.9 billion to $5.2 billion in such maintenance costs over the original F-100 engine. This line of reasoning led the Air Force to testify that "we have verified our projection of 2 to 3 billion dollar savings," over the estimated cost of $19.4 billion for the unimproved F-100.[23] Left unsaid is that these maintenance savings might have been achieved without the competition because of the more than $500 million in CIP funds spent on improving the reliability of the F-100. In addition, the stated savings resulting from the competition did not reflect the $400 million cost to qualify the F-110 as a competitive fighter engine.

2. The Air Force chose to split the award. The table shows that the split will cost approximately $1 billion *more* than a sole-source award to either P&W or GE. Part of this difference is due to the way in which the

21. See *Department of Defense Appropriations for Fiscal 1983*, Hearings, pt. 4, pp. 64–103.

22. The argument was not persuasive enough to stop the Air Force competition. P&W did not object when the Navy subsequently put GE in P&W's shoes by qualifying P&W as an alternative producer of GE's F-404 fighter engine for the Navy's F-18.

23. *Defense Department Authorization and Oversight*, Hearings on H.R. 5167, pt. 2, pp. 255, 225.

**Table 2-2. Air Force Analysis of Alternative Procurements for Fighter Engines**
Billions of fiscal 1983 dollars unless otherwise specified

| Contract award | Cost to government | Savings relative to a split award | |
|---|---|---|---|
| | | Amount | Percent |
| *Six annual purchases* | | | |
| Split | 17.32 | . . . | . . . |
| All to Pratt & Whitney | 16.39 | 0.93 | 5.3 |
| All to General Electric | 16.25 | 1.07 | 6.2 |
| *One purchase followed by five annual purchases* | | | |
| Split | 16.90 | . . . | . . . |
| All to Pratt & Whitney | 15.99 | 0.91 | 5.4 |
| All to General Electric | 15.74 | 1.16 | 6.9 |

Source: *Defense Department Authorization and Oversight*, Hearings on H.R. 5167 before the Committee on Armed Services, 98 Cong. 2 sess. (GPO, 1984), pt. 2, p. 255.

contractors priced their warranties, offering large savings for a 100 percent award. If there was a price advantage to be realized through competition, the Air Force sacrificed some of it to maintain two sources.

One can only speculate about what really drove the competition. Reducing program cost was not a factor because the Air Force chose the more expensive split award, and the savings in reliability might have been realized from the F-100 CIP program alone. Improved quality is also a difficult case to make in view of the fact that subsequent to the competition GE's monthly progress payments were suspended when the Air Force found quality control to be seriously deficient in the GE plant.[24] Maintaining the industrial base was not the rationale, since GE certainly was not lacking for military engine business. Indeed, splitting part of the F-15/F-16 engine business away from P&W could make P&W less competitive in the commercial business because of higher fixed costs per engine, as was argued by P&W. Perhaps the competition was motivated by military considerations alone, as argued in congressional testimony by Air Force General Robert D. Russ after the competition: "One of the things that drove us into this competition was the fact that we did not want to have almost our entire first-line fighter fleet with the same engine.

24. The irony is that P&W apparently had excellent quality control. Robert Waters, "Air Force Gives P&W Production High Grade," *Hartford Courant*, November 5, 1985, pp. D1, D2.

You can imagine what would happen if we had catastrophic failure of the hot section in the engine. The entire force would be grounded."[25]

### The U.S. Shipbuilding Industry

In comparison with other defense industries, the U.S. shipbuilding industry has some unique aspects.[26] It has long been almost wholly dependent on government subsidies and orders for its existence. Each ship takes years to build and its cost can exceed the book value of the shipyard. Shipyards normally do not maintain technical staffs but rely on architect-engineer firms to support ship design and construction.[27] As a result, 80 percent of a ship-yard's employees are production workers, as opposed to 48 percent in typical defense manufacturing facilities.[28] Both commercial and military shipbuilding tend to be highly cyclical.

Another unique feature of the industry is the financing method that has evolved for naval ship construction. Progress payments are based on contract price and the physical progress of the ship's construction, a concept fundamentally different from the normal DOD scheme, which is based on costs incurred, not physical progress. As a result, when a ship is being built near or below contracted costs, shipbuilders can theoretically receive progress payments in excess of their costs. For example, progress payments in fiscal 1983 were 96 percent of shipbuilders' current assets, compared with 61 percent for the rest of DOD procurements.[29] An efficient shipyard with a reasonable contract price for a naval ship could theoretically finance expenses entirely through progress payments and earn bank interest on the surplus. In contrast, defense contractors in other industries must finance work in process, with the interest charges paid out of their profit margin. Shipbuilding has a low rate of profit on sales (about 1.5 percent versus 7 percent for the rest of the defense industry), but when profit is added to imputed interest with government financing, shipbuilding

---

25. *Department of Defense Appropriations for 1986,* Hearings, pt. 6, p. 295.

26. For a discussion of the unique characteristics and financing of ship acquisition, see the shipbuilding section of U.S. Department of Defense, *Defense Financial and Investment Review,* June 1985, chap. 8. (Hereafter *DFAIR.*)

27. An excellent exposition of the current health of the shipbuilding industry can be found in Earl B. Fowler, Jr., "Competition Has the Potential for Major Impact on the Industry," in *The Almanac of Seapower, 1986* (Arlington, Va.: Navy League of the United States, 1986).

28. Gansler, *Defense Industry,* p. 192.

29. *DFAIR,* p. viii-1.

has the highest profit margins (before interest and taxes) of any defense industry (22 percent versus 12 percent).[30]

The U.S. shipbuilding industry is shrinking because of declining business—for example, the number of commercial ships under construction declined from ninety-six in 1975 to ten in 1985 to zero in 1988.[31] The U.S. Navy now accounts for 90 percent of revenue and employment in the shipbuilding industry. Despite the naval buildup launched by the Reagan administration in 1981, however, 25 of 110 U.S. shipyards closed between 1981 and 1985.[32]

The industry is highly concentrated, with only a few shipyards involved in construction. Overhaul and repair is divided among the many small yards as well as among the construction yards. The twenty-three active construction yards are fairly evenly distributed along U.S. shorelines: seven on the East Coast, eight on the Gulf of Mexico, five on the West Coast, and three on the Great Lakes.[33] Two of the yards, the Newport News Shipbuilding and Drydock division of Tenneco and the Electric Boat division of the General Dynamics Corporation, employ half the total labor force and are the only yards currently certified for construction of nuclear ships. Major conventionally powered surface combatants such as cruisers and destroyers are constructed in only three yards, whereas auxiliary and amphibious ships can be constructed in eight or more yards. Very little overlap exists among these three markets.

Data on ship prices and the procedures for calculating competitive savings are generally not available outside the Department of the Navy. Some of the calculations of savings appear to arise from internal Navy estimates of sole-source prices that were higher than bid prices received for new ship construction contracts. For example, the Perry Class (FFG-7) guided-missile frigate is frequently cited as a prime beneficiary of competition. In 1984 Vice Admiral Earl Fowler, then the commander of the Naval Sea Systems Command, told Congress, "We have saved more than $100 million on the first-fifteen follow ships of the Perry Class guided missile frigates. These are real savings because the price of each of these

30. *DFAIR*, pp. viii-6–viii-8.

31. M. Lee Rice, "Shipbuilding: Adrift in the Absence of a Clear-Cut National Policy," in *Almanac of Seapower, 1985* (Arlington, Va.: Navy League of the United States, 1985), p. 73.

32. Jonathan P. Hicks, "The Long Shipyard Slump," *New York Times*, November 15, 1985, pp. D1, D5.

33. Fowler, "Competition Has the Potential for Major Impact," p. 79.

ships was arrived at by competition among three good yards.''[34] However, the FFG-7 program has been under competition from the beginning. As a result, no sole-source history exists by which to measure competitive savings. Further, Admiral Fowler subsequently pointed out that West Coast yards have higher labor rates than East Coast and Gulf Coast yards and are not as efficient.[35] If the lowest bid price had been used to determine contract award, Bath Iron Works Corporation, a Maine yard, would have built the entire class because of its labor cost advantage over its two West Coast competitors, the Los Angeles division and the Seattle division of Todd Pacific Shipyards Corporation.[36]

A similar calculation, a competitive bid price compared with an estimate of a sole-source price, appears to have been made in the case of the Arleigh Burke class (DDG-51) guided-missile destroyer. The Navy has claimed that the fiscal 1985 competitive savings on the DDG-51 was $182 million.[37] Fiscal 1985 was the award year for the lead ship, so no sole-source price experience exists.

Two current ship programs have had a sole-source lead yard, the Ticonderoga class (CG-47) guided-missile cruiser, and the Whidbey Island class (LSD-41) dock-landing ship. The CG-47 class was initially a sole-source award to Ingalls shipbuilding division in Pascagoula, Mississippi; awards were subsequently split with Bath Iron Works. This competition led to bid prices for fiscal 1984 ships that were $100 million lower than the bid prices for the fiscal 1983 ships, and an additional $154.4 million savings for the fiscal 1985 ships.[38] Similarly, the first three ships of the LSD-41 class were awarded to Lockheed Shipbuilding on the West Coast, with the next three ships awarded to Avondale Shipyards on the Gulf Coast. Competitive savings on the LSD-41 program have been reported as $11 million.[39]

Other ship construction programs have not fared as well despite the use of competition. The mine countermeasures (MCM) program autho-

---

34. *Department of Defense Authorization for Appropriations for Fiscal Year 1985*, Hearings before the Senate Committee on Armed Services, 98 Cong. 2 sess. (GPO, 1984), pt. 8, p. 4177.

35. Fowler, ''Competition Has the Potential for Major Impact,'' p. 81.

36. Knowledgeable people in the ship costing business estimate the labor cost differential between some East Coast and West Coast yards can be in excess of 25 percent.

37. *Department of Defense Appropriations for 1986*, Hearings, pt. 4, p. 459.

38. *Department of Defense Appropriations for 1985*, Hearings before a Subcommittee of the House Committee on Appropriations, 98 Cong. 2 sess. (GPO, 1984), pt. 6, p. 474; and *Department of Defense Appropriations for 1986*, Hearings, pt. 4, p. 459.

39. *Department of Defense Appropriations for 1986*, Hearings, pt. 4., p. 459.

rized fourteen ships, and initial awards were made to two Wisconsin shipyards, Peterson Builders and Marinette Marine. The lead ship was delivered in 1985 by Peterson, eighteen months late and "millions of dollars over its $70 million budget."[40]

The two largest yards, Newport News and Electric Boat, have competed for nuclear-powered submarine construction. Newport News is the only facility capable of building nuclear-powered aircraft carriers, while Electric Boat has been the sole source for Trident submarines. The Navy is qualifying Newport News as a second source for the Trident. The Navy claimed $2.4 billion in savings from competition for the nuclear attack submarines (SSNs) between fiscal 1982 and 1984, and an additional $76.2 billion in fiscal 1985.[41] The perturbations in the SSN competition may not have lowered prices as much as possible. For example, when the Navy placed a freeze on business with Electric Boat in 1981 because of a dispute on the costs of contracted submarines, Newport News immediately raised its bid prices for a three-submarine contract that year. The negotiated price was $229 million a ship, up $52 million from the inflation-adjusted price of $177 million for the previous SSN award to Newport News. This increase in the level of SSN prices was claimed by some to have set a much higher level for all subsequent submarine contracts despite the reinstatement of Electric Boat as a competitive bidder.[42]

The results of competition are also unclear in the ship repair business. An examination by the General Accounting Office of seventy-five fixed-price contracts for ship repair revealed that all seventy-five ended up costing more than the contract price, by an average of 63 percent.[43] The Navy has acknowledged that this highly competitive market had led many to deliberately buy into a repair with a low bid and then attempt to recover on growth work and new work. The Navy maintains that these problems have diminished over the last several years.

The excess capacity of the U.S. shipbuilding industry has given the Navy some competitive gains, but it is not clear that all-out competition

40. The MCM case is described in Steven Eisenstadt, "Minesweeper Bids Killed; New 'Best Offers' Sought," *Navy Times*, February 17, 1986, p. 45.

41. John F. Fitzgerald, "Sub Costs Reported Up after Crackdown at EB," *Newark Star-Ledger*, January 15, 1986, p. 3; and *Department of Defense Appropriations for 1986*, Hearings, pt. 4, p. 459.

42. Fitzgerald, "Sub Costs Reported Up," p. 3.

43. Fred Hiatt, "Chronic Abuses Found in Navy Repair Program," *Washington Post*, February 11, 1986, p. A15.

is the preferred method of contracting. Calculations on competitive savings without a sole-source baseline to measure against and disappointing results on some competitive ship programs have clouded the picture. Indeed, competition may be the wrong procurement strategy for this industry, as noted by now-retired Vice Admiral Fowler: "The industrial base to support mobilization will be reduced further, and little will be done to slow its reduction. . . . Recent administrations have permitted the competitive market to establish the industrial base, and this is not likely to change."[44]

44. Fowler, "Competition Has the Potential for Major Impact," p. 81.

# CHAPTER THREE

# A DIFFERENT WAY TO LOOK AT COMPETITION

THE PRICE improvement curve model fails to yield any insight into the potential impact of competition for an acquisition program being considered for competition. For example, it fails to explain how sixteen of seventeen lead contractors for systems examined in the IDA 74 study—despite their theoretical price advantage arising from labor learning—lost to second sources in winner-take-all competitions for reprocurement.[1] Either the lead contractor was grossly inefficient or many more elements are at play in a competition environment than can be addressed with a single-parameter model. Whereas most studies of competition have focused primarily on aggregate price levels and not on such elements of price as overhead, labor, and materials, this chapter offers a different approach, disaggregating the elements of cost and examining contractor-specific overhead behavior. This alternative model provides a framework for analysis of a proposed hybrid competitive strategy that more closely aligns industry incentives with government interests.

## A Point of Departure

Currently the most comprehensive procedure for assessing a proposed competitive acquisition is that used within the Cost Analysis Improvement Group (CAIG) of the Office of the Secretary of Defense. The CAIG bases its procedure on the price improvement curve but includes adjustments for the nonrecurring costs of production such as fixed overhead and the

1. Morris Zusman and others, "A Quantitative Examination of Cost-Quantity Relationships: Competition during Procurement, and Military versus Commercial Prices for Three Types of Vehicles," IDA Paper S-429, vol. 2 (Arlington, Va.: Institute for Defense Analyses, March 1974).

costs of a duplicate set of tooling.[2] It is a break-even approach (in present-value terms) that projects the total recurring cost of continuing with a sole-source supplier and compares it with the sum of the investment required to establish a second source (including the cost of educational and qualification purchases at low rates of production) and the total recurring costs with two suppliers. In this scheme the second source must offer prices low enough to compensate for the nonrecurring costs expended by the government to establish the second source.

The CAIG method has several serious weaknesses. First, the projection of sole-source prices from early production runs could be very misleading because of the problems pointed out by Cullen. This is compounded by the additional problem of sorting out nonrecurring costs for early lots at the aggregate price level.[3] Second, assessing the reasonableness of receiving the required price from the second source is exceptionally difficult because historical data on analogous systems required for such an assessment are rare. It can easily lead to an anecdotal rather than a systematic basis for decisionmaking. Third, the CAIG methodology accepts the ''shift and rotate'' hypothesis, which also forces the examination toward anecdotal arguments (see chapter 1). However, a virtue of the methodology is its consideration of fixed costs at the competing firms, which requires knowledge of these costs at specific defense contractors and how they change under the influence of competition and variations in the business base. When lacking firm-specific data on fixed costs, however, the CAIG methodology assumes that, on average, 15 percent of unit price is essentially fixed overhead. If used for both contractors, this assumption masks the important potential price difference rooted in fixed costs. The difference in fixed costs between two firms can yield a price difference greater than differences in labor productivity and in willingness to take a reduced profit to win a contract.

### Contractor Incentives

Most reports on contractor behavior in the defense marketplace have been surveys and case studies in management journals. In a survey by the

2. Milton A. Margolis, Raymond G. Bonesteele, and James L. Wilson, ''A Method for Analyzing Competitive, Dual Source Production Programs,'' Office of the Secretary of Defense, Cost Analysis Improvement Group, n.d.

3. J. S. Cullen, ''Cost Estimating from Initial Actuals,'' paper prepared for the Office of the Director, Planning and Evaluation, Office of the Secretary of Defense, August 20, 1976.

U.S. Army Procurement Office in 1981, contractors were asked to identify their motivations.[4] The following responses were received, listed in their overall order of priority:

—provide a good product;

—have a long-term government relationship;

—improve cash flow;

—make a profit;

—develop new capabilities;

—maintain a positive public image;

—use excess capacity.

While it is difficult to make adjustments for the expression of self-interest in the respondents' choice of responses, the fact that profit was only the fourth priority is interesting. In a later 1984 survey, chief executive officers of Air Force contractors were asked, ''What incentives are likely to induce the defense industry to improve productivity with new facilities and equipment?'' The overwhelming response was ''stability.''[5]

If these results are at all credible, they strongly suggest that contractors have these strong, twin concerns: full utilization of present facilities for *current business,* and the generation of cash for technology and productivity advances sufficient to compete for *future business.* These concerns translate into actions that reflect a firm's business strategy and corporate culture. Knowledge of corporate culture is increasingly important because corporations often have strong biases toward certain business practices that only strong external influences can alter.[6] Defense acquisition managers currently view competition as such an external factor; this may be valid, but the incentives and behavior of specific firms must be understood

4. Robert F. Williams and Daniel M. Carr, ''Contractor Motivation Theory and Applications,'' ARPO 80-06 (Fort Lee, Va.: Army Procurement Research Office, March 1981).

5. Report on the 1984 U.S. Air Force Systems Command CEO Conference, June 6, 1984.

6. An example of a strong external catalyst for a major realignment of manufacturing strategy was the Boeing experience in 1970, when the commercial aircraft business nearly collapsed. The following story appears in John Newhouse, *The Sporty Game* (Knopf, 1982), pp. 169–70: ''In 1970, Boeing decimated its ranks at all levels: under a crash program, senior executives and engineers were let go, as well as the larger part of the company's highly skilled labor force. In mid-1968, the number of Boeing employees in the Seattle area reached a high of more than 101,000. Three years later, the figure had dropped to just above 37,000. . . . In making do with less, the company found, for example, that a labor force as large as it once had was neither essential nor desirable, even at times of high production rates. One study showed that a typical Boeing worker was actually at his station only 26 percent of the time; most of his shift was spent in finding tools and parts and doing similar chores. By relocating tools and parts and centralizing similar types of work, a Boeing executive estimated that the actual working time of

if the government is to reduce program costs and maintain an adequate industrial base. A successful government acquisition strategy should align the motivations of specific contractors with the government's best interest.[7]

### Short-Term Behavior in the Aerospace Industry

How does a major aerospace contractor respond to a changing business base? The following averages of distribution of costs within the business base of seven major aerospace contractors in 1982 is fundamental to the answer (figures are rounded):

| Component | Percent |
| --- | --- |
| Total materials | 52 |
| Raw materials and purchased parts | 32 |
| Subcontract | 20 |
| Total direct labor | 15 |
| Manufacturing | 9 |
| Engineering | 6 |
| Total overhead | 34 |
| Indirect labor | 10 |
| Fringe benefits | 11 |
| Facility cost and data processing | 7 |
| R&D and corporate office allocation | 3 |
| Other | 3 |

employees was increased to 70 percent." To get a good overview of the subject of external factors needed to alter corporate culture, see Jay W. Lorsch, "Managing Culture: The Invisible Barrier to Strategic Change," *California Management Review,* vol. 28 (Winter 1986), pp. 95–109.

7. In what is perhaps the only statistical attempt to analyze contractor behavior, Greer and Liao attempted to model the savings or loss arising from competition in seven different missile systems as a function of the annual average capacity utilization for the aerospace industry as a whole at the time of the competition. The hypothesis was that competition generates savings when there is low utilization—that is, the contractors are hungry—and could cost money when business is brisk. Although a plausible hypothesis, it was not supported in four of the seven systems. The model might well have been a better predictor if the capacity utilization for the competing firms themselves had been used, but the data were not available to the authors. See Willis R. Greer, Jr., and Shu S. Liao, *Cost Analysis for Dual-Source Weapon Procurement,* NPS54-83-011, report prepared for Chief of Naval Research (Monterey, Calif.: U.S. Department of the Navy, Naval Post Graduate School, October 1983).

Most of the subcategories shown above are self-explanatory.[8] The difference between purchased parts and subcontract work is that the former are typically items a contractor would not make (for example, brakes and wheels for aircraft); subcontracting covers assemblies that the prime could make but chose not to (for example, aircraft wings), or non-airframe equipment such as radars and fire control systems. Fringe benefits are for both the direct and indirect labor force. The facility costs cover insurance, maintenance, depreciation, taxes, and utilities. R&D costs consist of independent research and development and bid and proposal costs. "Other" covers a host of small expenses including communications, travel, and supplies.

The above distribution represents an average; variations between firms, such as different policies about what to make and what to buy, affect this distribution, so data that are specific to the firm should be used when available. Further, understanding how the distribution of these costs changes as a function of business base and of time is important to understanding the influence of competition on the behavior of contractors.

The first point to note is that half of a contract's value (52 percent) represents materials generated outside the plant of the prime contractor—that is, by vendors and subcontractors. Thus if a prime contractor is effectively managing its vendor base and has obtained reasonable prices from vendors, a competing prime contractor could hardly be expected to offer a significantly better price with a different set of inexperienced vendors and subcontractors. Indeed, a competing contractor could seek the same vendors to take advantage of their experience. Conversely, if the second prime has excess plant capacity and is more efficient than the subcontractors used by the first prime, it could gain some competitive advantage by making more and subcontracting less than the original prime contractor, thereby avoiding the extra layer of profit inherent in subcontract effort.

Second, the distribution of costs shows a relatively low share represented by manufacturing labor—9 percent of direct cost plus another 4 percent for fringe benefits, for a total of 13 percent. Thus arguments that an experienced, productive manufacturing labor force contributes much to a difference in contract price under competition are not credible. Even

8. The proprietary nature of the data prohibit the identification of the firms represented. The data update those based on three aerospace firms in Steve J. Balut, "Redistributing Fixed Overhead Costs," *Concepts: The Journal of Defense Systems Acquisition Management,* vol. 4 (Spring 1981), pp. 63–76.

if the competitor's direct labor force were 20 percent more productive, it would contribute only a 2.6 percent (direct labor plus fringe benefits) reduction in total price. Indeed, the relatively small size of the direct manufacturing labor portion suggests that government investment to improve labor productivity (such as the Industrial Modernization Incentive Program) has limited potential for dramatic savings to the government.[9]

Overhead is the least understood category of cost because firms, considering it to be extremely sensitive, make special efforts to keep it private. Overhead as a percentage of both value added and of overall manufacturing costs has been rising steadily for more than 100 years. Concurrently, the ratio of direct labor costs to value added has declined.[10]

One reason for the expanding share of overhead has been the growth in the number of exchanges of information necessary for production, known as transactions. Transactions include the ordering, receiving, and distributing of materials, the derivation of labor demand forecasts and production plans, certification that such transactions take place, and updates to the basic manufacturing schedule and procedures to accommodate changes in delivery schedule and design. The number of transactions for a production program is much less sensitive to the quantity of output than the amount of direct labor and materials is. The indirect labor force processes these transactions. One study estimates that change transactions represent 20 percent to 40 percent of overhead costs in electronics manufacturing.[11] A stable, long-term production program, such as a multiyear procurement with no engineering change orders during the course of the contract, could have significantly reduced the number of transactions required for production compared with a less stable program, and thus would require less indirect labor to support the manufacturing process. For example, one time ordering of materials for a four-year production run would reduce the number of such transactions required for four single-year buys by 75 percent.

Two other contributions to the growth of overhead have been the replacement of direct labor with automated manufacturing facilities and sophisticated capital equipment, and the increase in data processing requirements to support computer-aided design (CAD) and computer-aided

9. A comprehensive description of the incentive program can be found in Paul Schreiber, "Cutting Defense Costs," *Newsday*, September 22, 1985, p. 84.

10. Jeffrey G. Miller and Thomas E. Vollmann, "The Hidden Factory," *Harvard Business Review*, vol. 63 (September–October 1985), pp. 142–50.

11. Miller and Vollmann, *Hidden Factory*, p. 146.

manufacturing (CAM). The long-term implication of these trends is that recurring manufacturing costs will continue to diminish as a percentage of total cost. Significant labor costs could be sunk by the time production begins.[12] The high fixed costs to set up and sustain a production line will make high volume more attractive because it allocates these costs over a greater quantity—splitting a production program between two sources to sustain competition could be very costly given these trends.

Long-term trends in the overhead accounts are receiving intensive analysis by the Institute for Defense Analyses (IDA) under the sponsorship of the Office of the Secretary of Defense CAIG. Of more importance here is the short-term, fixed-cost behavior of a firm when faced with changes to its business base. These fixed expenses can be defined as those management will not want to vary in response to short-term phenomena.[13] They include plant and capital equipment costs and some portion of the indirect force. In the extreme, of course, all costs are variable. A decision to shut down or sell an entire facility would put fixed costs at zero; at the other end of the spectrum, the fixed costs of a firm with a dramatically increasing volume of business will grow slowly relative to volume until production approaches three full shifts and the physical limits of plant capacity. The firm will then be faced with the decision whether to acquire additional space and equipment, which represent new fixed expenses for the short term.

How much of the price in a contract represents fixed costs? A study by Balut analyzed the overhead accounts for three major aerospace contractors and determined that about 45 percent of their overhead was fixed relative to short-term variations in the business base that ranged from − 17 percent to 85 percent.[14] To see the implications of this result, recall that, in general, overhead accounts for 34 percent of a prime contractor's costs. One could also assume this to be true for the subcontractors as well. As a result, 41 percent of an end-item's price is overhead (34 percent of the

---

12. Another implication of the replacement of manufacturing labor with automated and computer-oriented facilities is gradual obsolescence of traditional management information and accounting systems. Geared today toward measuring direct labor hours as the basis for calculating productivity and price, the current systems will fail to provide management with insight into the dominant costs in an automated facility. For example, see Robert S. Kaplan, "Yesterday's Accounting Undermines Production," *Harvard Business Review,* vol. 62 (July–August 1984), pp. 95–101.

13. For a further explanation of fixed costs, see Jack Hirshleifer, "The Firm's Cost Function: A Successful Reconstruction?" *Journal of Business,* vol. 35 (July 1962), pp. 235–55.

14. Balut, "Redistributing Fixed Overhead Costs," p. 70.

prime effort and 34 percent of the 20 percent subcontracted effort). If 45 percent of this overhead is fixed, as suggested in the Balut study, then 18 percent (45 percent of 41 percent) of the end-item's price is fixed in the short term. (Recall the CAIG assumption that 15 percent of recurring price is fixed cost.) The compelling conclusion of this calculation is that a doubling of the production volume would result in a reduction of 9 percent in price (half of 18 percent), without even considering the learning curve savings arising from the greater quantity.

Additional cost data on a greater number of aerospace firms have become available since Balut's study.[15] The expanded data base shows that on average more than 50 percent of overhead is fixed in the short term—the share of percentages ranges roughly from 50 percent to 70 percent. Making the calculation in the preceding paragraph with this newer data indicates that 21 to 29 percent (versus 18 percent) of an end-item's price is fixed in the short term. One would be hard pressed to ignore the potential cost savings of 10 to 15 percent from increases in volume compared with the costs of developing a second contractor and splitting a planned procurement just to achieve competition.

An additional and important insight from this new data is that, although engineering labor is usually considered to vary directly with plant volume, it may not. Figure 3-1 shows the engineering labor expended as a function of the in-house base (total business base less material, or "conversion," costs) for five major aerospace contractors. Two of the contractors (A and B) have sustained a relatively stable business base either by subcontracting out or by taking work inside as their overall business base varied. The other three (C, D, and E) have had much more variation in in-house effort. Although the sample size is small, the data suggest corporate strategies to protect the stock of engineering talent. Firms A and B have allowed less than a 30 percent variation in their engineering work force. Firm C, a high-growth corporation, has used its increasing business base to establish an engineering team comparable in size to that of A and B. Firms D and E, which have seen major swings in in-house production volume, have allowed the size of their engineering work force to change less than 25 percent, despite a halving and doubling of volume during the time frame considered. The data suggest that firms must retain a certain minimum number of engineers to remain competitive for new design awards,

15. Additional data have been collected by the Institute of Defense Analyses under CAIG sponsorship.

**Figure 3-1. The Variation in Engineering Labor with the Business Base at Five Aerospace Firms**

Thousands of engineering worker years

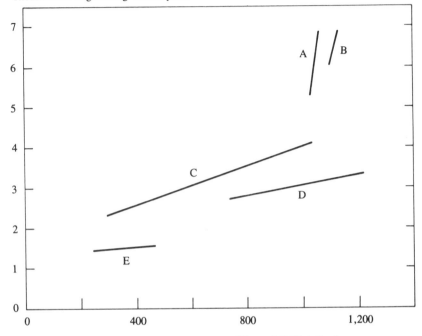

Annual in-house business base (millions of 1982 dollars)

Source: Proprietary data collected by IDA under the sponsorship of the OSD CAIG.

even if it means moving engineers to the indirect-labor side of the ledger as volume declines. Informal exchanges with aerospace industry officials support this conclusion, and it is also consistent with the survey data presented at the beginning of this chapter.

## A Competition Model

The extensive overhead data collected by the IDA offer the opportunity to construct firm-specific models that will capture an individual firm's overhead characteristics. These models could help policymakers decide whether to commit nonrecurring investments in a second source to introduce competition into an acquisition program. The overhead data clearly separate firms whose corporate strategy is to maintain a stable in-house work force from growth firms and from those that vary the size of the work force (often out of necessity) as their overall business varies. The essence of the model proposed here is to calculate the costs of the direct manufacturing effort separately; this is a relatively straightforward task, given the extensive firm-specific data available within DOD and the costs of the indirect efforts based on IDA firm-specific data on overhead cost.

The details of the IDA overhead models remain unpublished for proprietary reasons. For the purposes of the competition cost model proposed here, the following description should suffice. The functional form of a firm-specific overhead model is

$$X = a + bK + cL,$$

where $X$ is total overhead dollars in a given year, $K$ is the capital stock value for that year, and $L$ is direct manufacturing labor dollars.[16] Dummy variables are occasionally used to capture unique characteristics such as changes in a firm's accounting scheme during the period covered by the data. The regression coefficients are represented by the terms $a$, $b$, and $c$. The regression intercept, $a$, can be thought of as the true fixed costs of a facility. But because the value for $a$ is outside the range of the data, this characterization is pedagogical rather than analytic. The regression term $bK$ represents the portion of semifixed costs that are fixed in the short term. Direct labor, $L$, is assumed to be completely variable. The short-term fixed cost percentage for a given year is calculated as

$$\frac{a + bK}{X}.$$

Note that the term fixed is a misnomer in that $K$ does vary with manufacturing activity. The problem here, however, is not to calculate fixed costs but to integrate the overhead cost model into a larger model for use in deciding whether to introduce competition.

The essence of the procedure would be, first, to estimate direct manufacturing effort for a sole-source manufacturer, using either that firm's specific learning curve performance, or early manufacturing performance on similar hardware if the item in question is not yet in production. Add to the manufacturing effort the sum of the estimated overhead costs for each year of production. The second step would be to make the comparable

16. This technique and functional form for fixed-cost calculations were jointly developed by the cost analysis organization at the Institute of Defense Analyses and CAIG.

calculations for an additional producer being considered, either as a second production facility or as a head-to-head competitor in a winner-take-all competition. This would capture the diminished learning-curve progress because of dual-production lines, the allocation of different overhead structures to the respective production lines, and the calculation of the nonrecurring costs of qualifying an additional producer. With the results in hand, a policymaker could then evaluate the reasonableness of additional producers realistically competing with the initial producer and make an informed decision on whether to commit the nonrecurring investment required. The disparity may appear too great; for example, the model may show that a second source might have to forgo any profit and have substantially lower overhead costs per unit than that producer's overhead history indicates in order to bid competitively. In that case, a policymaker would have some justification for continuing with a sole-source procurement. The appendix to this chapter offers a detailed example of this technique.

### Policy Implications and Some Recommendations

Drastic cost-cutting actions by major aerospace contractors, which win contracts but which also mortgage the contractors' future capabilities, are not in the government's best interests if a broad and modern defense industrial base is desired. A partial solution to this dilemma has been to keep two competitors going with production of the same item. The contracts give each firm the resources it needs to sustain modern manufacturing capabilities and current engineering expertise. Although the competitive environment may offset some of the additional cost of carrying two contractors, little evidence exists that dual sourcing actually reduces program costs. Indeed, data in this chapter suggest that a split purchase is more likely to increase the costs for a project. Moreover, a guaranteed minimum purchase from both the competitors can reduce prices only if no collusion exists between them and both want to win the major share.[17]

17. In microeconomic theory, a true competitive environment with two firms reaches equilibrium only when one contractor assumes leadership and the other follows. If both want to be followers, equilibrium (and profit maximization) will obtain after each realizes the other wants to be a follower. If both want to be leaders, the situation is called a Stackelberg disequilibrium, which will continue until one firm has succumbed to the leadership of the other or a collusive agreement has been reached. A more detailed exposition can be found in James M. Henderson and Richard E. Quandt, *Microeconomic Theory: A Mathematical Approach* (McGraw-Hill, 1971). Application of this theory to the defense sector is discussed in Brent Meeker's "Second-

Otherwise, a crafty competitor could willingly opt for the smaller award and use it to generate cash flow and become more competitive in other product lines.

If dual sourcing has these negative aspects, what other options are there? Winner-take-all competitions offer the greatest opportunity to reduce costs.[18] However, they effectively eliminate the option for later competition if additional procurement is desired of the basic model or a follow-on design change to that model. An alternative is to continue competitions for fixed-price, winner-take-all multiyear contracts. The runner-up bidder in the competition would be awarded an engineering support contract for the design effort for the *next model* in the *same series* at the end of the multiyear procurement schedule. In addition, during production by the winner of the competition, the runner-up firm could be the integrating facility for all changes to the basic model. This activity would ensure that the runner-up firm would remain competitive and interested at the time of model change. Obviously, close oversight would be required to prevent the second firm from extensively redesigning the hardware in order to disadvantage the original winner.

One could argue that announcing a major production contract award to the winning bidder while at the same time awarding a contract to the second bidder for design of an improved model several years later is peculiar. In an era of constrained resources, why not just wait for the improved model and forgo the production of the basic model? The first answer is that the government may not have the choice. The new equipment may be needed to fill a critical, near-term requirement. A second point is that the government already makes simultaneous awards of production contracts and contracts to improve the design, but in a more limited fashion. Typically, design-improvement contracts are awarded not to the second bidder as proposed here but to the winning competitor. Under the current procedures, the losing bidders use their own funds and government funds where possible to propose totally new designs for follow-on systems rather than incremental improvements to the winning design, which would prove less costly to the government.

---

Source Splits: An Optimum Non-solution," *Program Manager*, vol. 13 (March–April 1984), pp. 2–8.

18. A point consistently made by Beltramo. See, for example, Michael N. Beltramo, "A Case Study of the Sparrow AIM-7F: Findings, Theories, and Thoughts about Competition in the Procurement of Weapon Systems," *Program Manager*, vol. 14 (September–October 1985), pp. 28–35.

The alternative approach offers the government the best features of the second-source strategy (maintain a viable competitor for future procurements) and winner-take-all competitions (aggressive pricing to win the production contract). The multiyear nature of the award guarantees program stability and its favorable effects. From the second contractor's perspective, the engineering design award preserves the integrity of its engineering design team. Holding a new competition at the point of model change offers the second firm a chance to compete more equitably—model changes result in a loss of labor learning for the original contractor on the portions that have been changed, thus putting both competitors at the beginning of the learning curve on some portions of the hardware. This strategy has the added advantage of forcing the development of derivative systems rather than radically new systems. Totally new designs typically incorporate several different technological advances simultaneously and thereby carry higher risks and costs than incrementally changed systems.

### Appendix: An Example of the Competition Model

In this example the government makes an initial sole-source procurement of 300 fighter aircraft, after which it wants follow-on production of 600 aircraft spread over five annual purchases.[19] Although the data and calculations are only illustrative of the proposed competition model, they are sufficiently meaningful to allow insight into the criteria by which to judge whether such a competition is beneficial and, if so, how best to conduct it.

The fighter has an airframe weight of 15,000 pounds. The prime contractor, Company A, has manufactured 60 percent of the frame (by weight) and performed all final assembly and integration. The major subcontractor, Company B, has manufactured the other 40 percent of the airframe. If only the final assembly and integration work is put out for competition, rather than the entire production effort, potential savings are small because final assembly and integration represent only about 20 percent of the direct manufacturing hours. Therefore, in this example 100 percent of the pro-

19. Such a situation arose when the Army qualified the Hellfire missile seeker subcontractor, Martin-Marietta, to compete as a prime contractor with the original prime, Rockwell. The Hellfire competition is described in detail in Analytic Sciences Corporation, "Competition during Army Weapon System Acquisition," Final Report, TR-4613-8-1 (Arlington, Va., June 21, 1985).

duction effort will be at stake, spread over a five-year multiyear procurement. The split of manufacturing effort among the categories of fabrication, subassembly, and final assembly varies as a function of the number of units. For ease of calculation, the ratio is assumed to remain constant throughout the life of the program.[20]

The competitive issue is whether the advantage in labor learning that A possesses on 60 percent of the frame and 100 percent of the final assembly could be offset by B's learning curve advantage on the other 40 percent of the frame and its more favorable overhead structure. Company A historically has chosen to maintain a relatively stable in-house workload by giving work to subcontractors or taking work back into the plant as its overall business base varied. Its plant is fully utilized. In contrast, B is a growth company that has used expansion of its business base to increase its capacity. Additional assumptions used in the calculations are as follows:

—The learning curve for direct manufacturing hours is a log linear cumulative average curve with a slope of 80 percent. Learning on the first 300 airframes has reduced the total manufacturing effort to ten man-hours per pound of airframe.

—The regression formulas for the overhead models of the two firms are:

$$X_A = 200 + 0.7K + 1.45L$$

$$X_B = 150 + 0.6K + 1.50L,$$

where $X$ is overhead in 1983 dollars for a given year, $K$ is the capital stock (net book value) of the plant in millions of dollars, and $L$ is the direct manufacturing labor dollars in millions of dollars. Current overhead for the two firms is as follows:

$$X_A = 200 + 0.7(700) + 1.45(200) = \$980,000,000$$

$$X_B = 150 + 0.6(600) + 1.50(100) = \$660,000,000.$$

—A given year's overhead is absorbed by the year's purchase of aircraft. Without this assumption, more detailed calculations would require

---

20. The split used can be found in Harold Asher, *Cost-Quantity Relationships in the Airframe Industry*, R-291 (Santa Monica, Calif.: Rand Corp., July 1, 1956), p. 69. Asher gives the following percents: fabrication, 24; subassembly, 35; major and final assembly, 41. In the example here, half the major and final assembly (20 percent) is assumed to be the final assembly and integration effort.

streaming the manufacturing effort over the longer period of initial fabrication, assembly, and then delivery time. The assumption does not affect the outcome.

—The fighter production represents 50 percent of the manufacturing effort at both A and B. For ease of calculation, the nonfighter work will be assumed to remain constant throughout the period.

—Both contractors are equally effective in negotiating with vendors for raw materials and purchased parts.

—The competition would be winner-take-all so that the existing tooling could be used by the winner and need not be duplicated.

—The cost of one direct manufacturing man-year is $25,000.

—The calculations below need only reflect differences in direct manufacturing costs and overhead costs to determine if the competition is a realistic one.

## Labor Hours

In the competition for 100 percent of the follow-up production of 600 airframes, each firm would start at the first unit on the learning curve for the work previously done at the other facility. Company A, in keeping with its previous corporate behavior and its full utilization of its plant, would choose to subcontract out the 40 percent of the work previously performed in Company B. It is also reasonable to assume that Company B would choose to take all the airframe manufacturing effort in-house because its plant is underutilized. The following table compares the millions of manufacturing man-hours each competitor would require in the winner-take-all competition for 600 airframes:

| Component | Company A | Company B |
|---|---|---|
| 40 percent of frame | 23.04 | 15.93 |
| 60 percent of frame | 23.89 | 34.56 |
| Final assembly | 9.95 | 14.40 |
| Total | 56.88 | 64.89 |

Company A requires 8 million fewer hours, for a direct-charge advantage of $100 million, or $20 million a year for a five-year program.

*Overhead*

The coefficients for the regression formulas indicate that the relatively fixed costs for A are higher than for B (the $a + bK$ component of the equation). However, because A is a larger firm, its elasticity coefficient for the labor variable, $L$, is lower than that for B; that is, overhead at A does not grow as much for a given increase in direct labor dollars. The critical parameters will be the firm-specific variables for capital stock, $Ka$ and $Kb$. Although a complete analysis on the variations of $K$ could be made, this example uses values for $K$ that reflect the typical behavior of actual firms similar to A and B. The variable $K$ would remain level at A if it won; if B won, it would rise by 10 percent at B to accommodate the growth in work. The fighter share of the $980 million overhead at A is $490 million; the fighter share of the resultant $926 million overhead at B is $743 million.

The effort on the 40 percent of the airframe that A subcontracts out will carry the overhead of the subcontractor; the profitability of A's subcontractor is similar to that of A itself. (A subcontractor with lower overhead could be assumed for actual applications of the model if the information is available to the analyst.) With these assumptions, the cost differences for a single year between A and B, in millions of dollars, are as follows:

| Component | Comapny A | Company B |
|---|---|---|
| Labor | 142 | 162 |
| Overhead | 490 | 743 |
| Subcontractor's overhead and profit | 164 | . . . |
| Total | 796 | 905 |

The difference (less profit) between the firms is $109 million in each year, approximately $1 million per airframe for the annual purchase of 120 aircraft. Assuming that an additional 32 percent of cost is for raw materials and purchased parts and a 10 percent profit rate for A, a $10.7 million unit cost would result. Firm B could duplicate this cost if it chose to bid with no profit in its offer, a realistic possibility in an era of constrained resources and decreasing numbers of major aircraft models in production.

*Other Applications*

The methodology could be used to determine the effect of a decision by A to expand its capacity in order to take all of the work in-house. This would increase the value of its capital stock and cause a larger share of overhead to be picked up by the fighter production.

Another application would be the evaluation of competition at the time of model changes. If A were to win the competition for the follow-on procurement of 600 aircraft and the government contemplated a model change midway through the reprocurement (the 600th airframe of the 900-aircraft program), would the government be completely at the mercy of A or could B provide realistic competition? The methodology proposed here provides a tool to evaluate such situations and could even calculate the changes in airframe weight that would be necessary before B could compete effectively.